# DAY TRADING FOR PERSONAL FREEDOM

## Vaibhav Jain

## Quit The 9-5 And Join me on a much more profitable path!

ISBN:9798858534013

Independently published

# STAY AHEAD, SURVIVE AND THRIVE

You want to be ahead of the crowd. You want to be in top 1% of Day Traders then buy this and do everything like the top 1% do. Find out your weaknesses and take my expert help to propel yourself ahead of the crowd. I am for a limited time willing to help all my readers an opportunity to reach out to me and change their lives forever and join an exclusive group of people with the same goal details at the end.

Day Trading For Personal Freedom is your guide to set you free from the grind and enable you earn ten times more than your job. Ten years ago I set out and I have achieved and can set you on a fast track path of success. Details of my group at the end.

# CONTENTS

# THE AMERICAN DREAM

I can say with confidence I have been able to achieve the American dream. I started from a very small village in India where they still live in mud houses and earn less than 100 dollars a month.

From graduating from a top university in India to coming to Wall Street and working for Morgan Stanley and living in New York city for many years I believed I had made it, but still thought something lacking, I yearned for personal freedom. I had saved for the past 12 years and I believed I could now earn much more than my job if I quit this and return to India.

Within a month I had packed my bags, given resignation and headed to India. It wasn't as rosy as it seemed, I fell on hard times, It took me a long 10 years to finally have everything ready and start making big bucks.

Now finally achieving the dream, I am here to help anyone shorten his path to success as a day trader and quit the 9-5.

# 1 THE BEAR STORY

In a tranquil corner of the dense forest, two friends, Jake and Ryan, decided to embark on a thrilling hike to reconnect with nature and create lasting memories. Little did they know that their adventure would soon take an unexpected turn.

The sun was casting dappled shadows through the thick canopy as the friends walked along a narrow trail. Their laughter filled the air as they shared stories and marvelled at the beauty around them. Suddenly, a rustling in the underbrush caught their attention. Jake's heart skipped a beat as he caught sight of a massive brown bear emerging from the foliage.

"Ryan, look!" Jake whispered urgently, nudging his friend and pointing toward the bear.

Ryan's eyes widened in both awe and alarm as he took in the majestic yet potentially dangerous creature. "Wow, that's incredible," he murmured, his voice tinged with nervousness.

Jake's pulse raced, and without hesitation, he turned to Ryan, his competitive spirit taking over. "I bet I can outrun you to that big oak tree up ahead," Jake declared, his eyes fixed on the distant tree as he subtly prepared to make a dash for it.

Ryan blinked at his friend in disbelief. "Are you crazy? We need to stay calm and back away slowly. Running might provoke the bear!"

But Jake was already off, his feet pounding the earth as he sprinted toward the oak tree. Ryan hesitated for a moment, torn between his competitive instincts and his better judgment. He watched in disbelief as Jake put distance between them, his figure growing smaller in the distance.

Meanwhile, the bear, sensing the sudden

movement, turned its attention toward Jake and the fleeing form. The bear's instincts kicked in, and it began to give chase.

"Jake, stop! It's not a race!" Ryan shouted, his voice echoing through the forest.

Jake's heart pounded as he reached the oak tree and looked back. He froze when he realized the bear was indeed gaining on him, its massive form covering the ground with surprising speed.

Ryan's voice reached his ears once more, this time laced with concern. "Lie down and play dead if it gets close, Jake!"

With a burst of adrenaline, Jake altered his course, heading for a fallen log nearby. He scrambled up onto the log and, following Ryan's advice, he curled into a fetal position and covered the back of his neck with his hands.

The bear skidded to a stop just shy of the log, huffing and snorting as it sized up the curious creature before it. The tension in the air was palpable as the bear assessed the situation.

Ryan arrived moments later, panting heavily from his exertion. The bear's attention shifted between the two men, its curiosity seemingly piqued by their contrasting responses.

For what felt like an eternity, the forest held its breath. Eventually, the bear seemed to lose interest, turning away from the log and lumbering back into the woods.

Relief washed over Jake and Ryan as they slowly rose to their feet. Jake's competitive streak had nearly cost him dearly, but it was also his swift thinking and Ryan's level-headedness that had kept them both safe.

"Next time," Ryan panted, his voice tinged with both amusement and concern, "let's just enjoy the hike without turning it into a race, okay?"

Jake chuckled weakly, his heart still racing. "Yeah, you're right. No more races with bears."

With that promise, the friends continued their hike, now sharing a newfound respect for the wilderness and the creatures that called it home. As they ventured deeper into the forest, their laughter returned, but their steps were more cautious, and the memory of their encounter with the bear remained etched in their minds—read this many times there are several layers of thoughts hidden in this. The thought is if you start losing then don't chase losses, if you have a habit of chasing losses

then start imaging you have no more left, play dead.
This is one thought, can you find more in the story?

# 2 CONTINUOUS EDUCATION SHARPENS THE KNIFE

Day trading, often touted as a fast-paced and exhilarating endeavour, holds the promise of substantial profits and financial independence. However, the road to success in the world of day trading is not paved with shortcuts or luck; rather, it is built upon a solid foundation of knowledge and continuous learning. In this cha, we will delve into the importance of continuously learning about trading strategies, technical analysis, market indicators, and trading psychology – all of which contribute to making informed decisions that can lead to day trading success.

## 1. Understanding Trading Strategies

At the heart of every successful day trader's toolkit lies a diverse range of trading strategies. These strategies are the blueprints that guide a trader's actions in the market, helping them identify potential entry and exit points. As a day trader, it is crucial to immerse yourself in various trading methodologies, from trend-following to momentum trading and scalping. By developing a comprehensive understanding of these strategies, you can adapt your approach to different market conditions and increase your chances of success.

## 2. Mastering Technical Analysis

Technical analysis serves as the bedrock of day trading. By studying price charts, patterns, and historical data, day traders can gain insights into potential market movements. Learning technical analysis allows you to identify trends, support and resistance levels, and chart patterns that can be exploited for profit. From moving averages to

Bollinger Bands, honing your technical analysis skills can greatly enhance your ability to make informed trading decisions.

### 3. Navigating Market Indicators

Market indicators are the compass that guides day traders through the ever-changing financial landscape. These tools provide invaluable insights into market sentiment, volatility, and potential price reversals. From Relative Strength Index (RSI) to Moving Average Convergence Divergence (MACD), understanding and effectively using market indicators can help you fine-tune your entry and exit points and optimize your risk management strategies.

### 4. Mastering Trading Psychology

While technical skills are crucial, an often-underestimated aspect of day trading success is mastering trading psychology. The ability to remain calm under pressure, manage emotions, and avoid impulsive decisions can make or break a trader. Continuous learning in this area involves understanding cognitive biases, developing a disciplined mindset, and implementing stress-reduction techniques. A strong foundation in trading psychology can help you navigate the emotional rollercoaster of trading and stay focused on your long-term goals.

# 3 PRESERVE CAPITAL STAY IN THE GAME

The fast-paced nature of the markets also carries inherent risks. To truly thrive in the world of day trading, one must not only seek opportunities but also prioritize the protection of their capital. In this chapter, we will explore the critical importance of implementing effective risk management strategies to safeguard your hard-earned capital. We'll delve into the concepts of setting stop-loss orders, defining position sizes based on risk tolerance, and the perils of overexposing yourself to a single trade.

1. **The Art of Stop-Loss Orders**

Stop-loss orders are your first line of defense in risk management. They act as a safety net, automatically triggering an exit from a trade when a predefined price level is reached. By setting stop-loss orders, day traders can limit potential losses and prevent a single unfavorable trade from severely impacting their capital. It is essential to determine stop-loss levels based on technical analysis, ensuring they are strategically placed to account for market volatility while also aligning with your risk tolerance.

2. **Position Sizing: Balancing Risk and Reward**

A cornerstone of effective risk management is position sizing. Before entering any trade, it's vital to calculate the appropriate position size based on your risk tolerance and the distance to your stop-loss level. Position sizing ensures that no single trade can wipe out a substantial portion of your capital. Striking the right balance between risk and reward is key, as overly large positions can lead to heart-wrenching losses, while excessively small positions may limit your potential profits.

3. **Diversification and Avoiding Overexposure**

In the quest for higher profits, day traders may be tempted to invest a significant portion of their capital in a single trade. However, overexposing yourself to a single trade is a perilous path that can lead to catastrophic losses. Diversification is the antidote to this risk. By spreading your capital across multiple trades and asset classes, you reduce the impact of a single unfavorable market movement. Diversification hedges against the inherent unpredictability of the markets and helps preserve your capital over the long term.

4. **Staying Disciplined: The Psychology of Risk Management**

Implementing risk management strategies isn't solely about numbers and formulas; it's also deeply intertwined with trading psychology. Staying disciplined and adhering to your risk management plan, even in the face of emotions like fear and greed, is essential. Emotional decision-making can lead to impulsive actions that deviate from your strategy and expose you to unnecessary risks. Maintain a strong mindset, recognize the importance of risk management, and remember that preservation of capital is a cornerstone of sustainable day trading success.

.

# 4 AVOIDING IMPULSIVE DECISIONS IS THE KEY

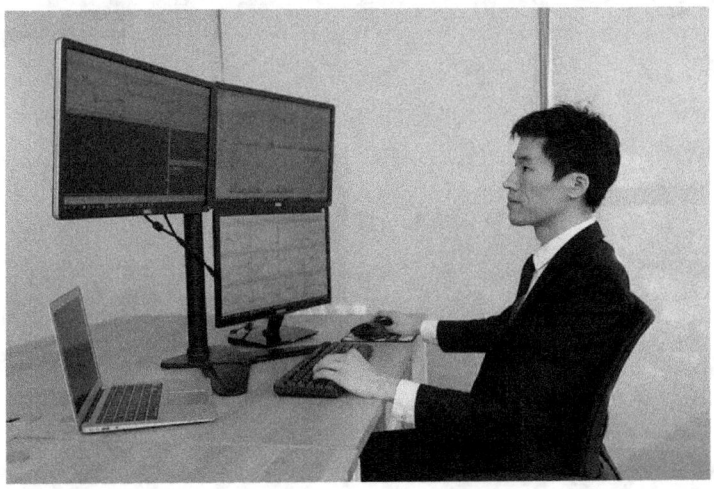

Beneath the surface of excitement lies a challenging reality: the need for unwavering discipline and emotional control. In this chapter, we will delve into the critical importance of developing strong discipline and emotional control for day traders. We will explore how these qualities help traders avoid impulsive decisions driven by fear or greed, stick to their trading plans, and ultimately steer clear of the pitfalls of chasing losses or deviating from their strategies.

## 1. Taming the Emotional Rollercoaster

The world of day trading is a constant interplay of emotions – fear, greed, excitement, and frustration. To succeed, day traders must learn to recognize and manage these emotions effectively. Impulsive decisions driven by fear can lead to premature exits or missed opportunities, while decisions fueled by greed can result in overexposure to risk. Developing emotional control requires self-awareness, mindfulness, and the ability to detach emotions from trading decisions.

## 2. The Power of a Trading Plan

A well-structured trading plan is a day trader's North Star. It serves as a roadmap, outlining entry and exit criteria, risk management rules, and overall strategies. Adhering to a trading plan minimizes the influence of emotions and reduces the likelihood of impulsive decisions. By thoroughly back testing and fine-tuning your plan, you can build confidence in its effectiveness and be better equipped to stay disciplined even in the face of market turbulence.

## 3. Avoiding the Temptation of Chasing Losses

Chasing losses, often driven by a desire to recoup losses quickly, is a dangerous trap that can lead to further losses. Developing discipline means accepting losses as part of the trading journey and resisting the urge to make impulsive trades in a desperate attempt to recover. Remember, trading decisions should be rational, informed by analysis, and aligned with your trading plan, rather than influenced by emotional reactions.

4. **Staying the Course and Resisting Deviation**

Consistency is the hallmark of disciplined day traders. Deviating from your established strategy can lead to confusion, erratic decision-making, and ultimately, losses. It's crucial to have the strength to resist the temptation to make impulsive changes during moments of uncertainty. Stick to your plan, remain patient, and trust the process you have meticulously designed.

5. **Mindset and Mindfulness**

Cultivating a disciplined mindset requires ongoing effort. Practicing mindfulness techniques, such as meditation or journaling, can help you stay centered and focused during trading hours. By training your mind to observe thoughts and emotions without reacting, you can make more rational and calculated decisions, free from the influence of impulsive reactions.

# 5 CREATE A ROBUST TRADING SYSTEM

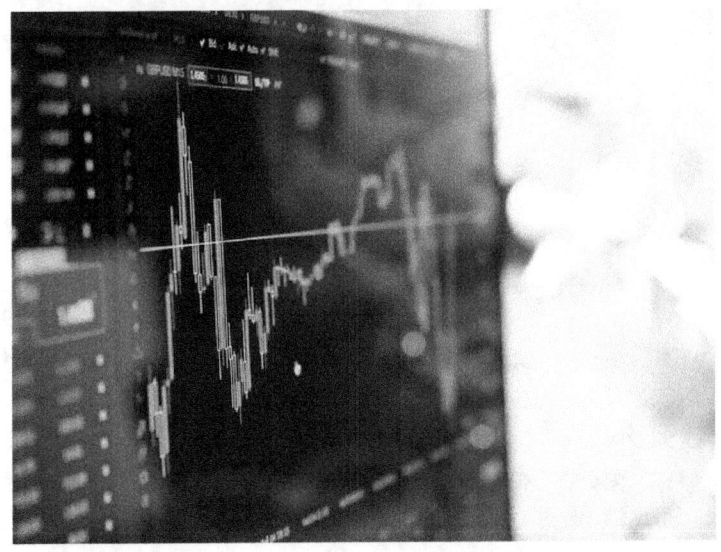

It necessitates a structured approach, one that is grounded in a well-defined trading plan. In this chapter, we will explore the integral role of a robust trading plan in the day trader's arsenal. We'll delve into the components that make up an effective plan – from setting clear goals and strategies to establishing risk management rules and entry/exit criteria. Moreover, we will emphasize the importance of regularly reviewing and adapting your plan to accommodate ever-changing market conditions and your own performance.

1. **Setting Clear Goals and Objectives**

A successful day trader begins their journey with a clear sense of purpose. What do you aim to achieve through day trading? Defining your financial goals – whether they involve consistent income, capital growth, or achieving a specific percentage return – will provide you with a guiding light as you navigate the complex world of markets.

2. **Strategizing for Success**

Your trading strategies are the tools that will help you achieve your goals. Whether you lean towards trend-following, momentum trading, or other techniques, it's crucial to articulate these strategies within your trading plan. Detail how you will identify potential trade setups, which indicators you'll rely on, and the timeframes you'll operate in. Having a clear strategy helps you maintain focus amidst market noise.

3. **Risk Management: The Guardian of Your Capital**

No trading plan is complete without robust risk management rules. Determine how much of your capital you're willing to risk on each trade, and establish appropriate position sizing based on your risk tolerance and stop-loss levels. This discipline safeguards your capital and helps you weather periods of volatility.

4. **Precise Entry and Exit Criteria**

Your trading plan should outline specific criteria for entering and exiting trades. Define the technical and fundamental factors that will trigger a trade entry, and establish clear rules for when to take profits or cut losses. By having well-defined entry and exit points, you minimize emotional decision-making and maintain consistency in your trading approach.

5. **Review and Adaptation: Staying Ahead of the Curve**

The financial markets are ever-evolving, and a static trading plan can quickly become obsolete. Regularly reviewing your plan enables you to assess its effectiveness in different market conditions. Take note of your performance – what's working, what's not, and what adjustments could improve your results. Be willing to adapt your strategies, risk management rules, and even your goals as your experience and the market landscape evolve.

### 6. The Power of Backtesting

Before implementing changes, consider backtesting your proposed adjustments using historical data. This helps you assess the potential impact of your modifications and refine your plan further.

# 6 BE FLEXIBLE OR GET BROKEN

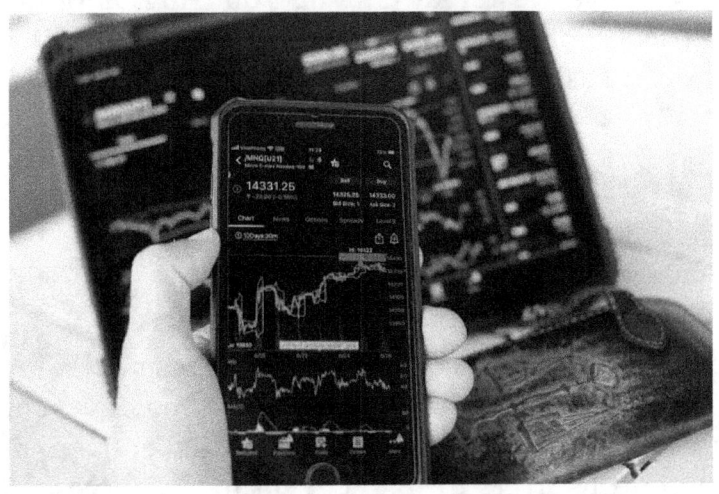

In this fast-paced arena, the ability to adapt and remain flexible is not just a virtue – it's a necessity. In this chapter, we will delve into the paramount importance of adaptability and flexibility for day traders. We'll explore how successful traders embrace the ever-changing nature of markets, adjust their strategies in response to evolving trends and breaking news, and ultimately carve their path to victory in the dynamic world of day trading.

## 1. The Fluid Nature of Markets

Markets are a living entity, influenced by an intricate web of economic indicators, geopolitical events, and investor sentiments. What works today may not work tomorrow, and what seemed predictable yesterday might suddenly defy all expectations. Recognizing this inherent dynamism is the first step to becoming an adaptable day trader.

## 2. Embracing Evolution: Adjusting Strategies

The hallmark of a seasoned day trader is their willingness to embrace change and adapt their strategies accordingly. Your chosen trading methodologies and technical analysis tools are your arsenal, but they must be versatile enough to respond to shifts in market sentiment. Successful traders are quick to recognize when a strategy is losing its edge and are unafraid to pivot to more relevant approaches.

## 3. The Role of Evolving Trends

Market trends can be as fleeting as they are lucrative. A trend that propelled your profits yesterday might reverse today. Adaptable day traders keep a watchful eye on evolving trends, allowing them to hop on the bandwagon at the right time and exit before it fizzles out. This requires staying informed, utilizing real-time data, and responding swiftly to shifts.

### 4. News as a Catalyst for Change

Breaking news can send shockwaves through the market, instantly altering its landscape. Adaptable day traders are voracious consumers of news, from economic reports to geopolitical developments. They understand that news can disrupt established patterns, and they're ready to adjust their positions or even exit trades when necessary to safeguard their capital.

### 5. The Flexibility of Risk Management

Flexibility in day trading extends beyond strategy adjustments – it also encompasses risk management. Adaptable traders understand that unexpected market movements can lead to unforeseen losses. They are proactive in setting appropriate stop-loss levels and adjusting position sizes to account for increased volatility.

### 6. Learning from Every Trade

Each trade is a learning opportunity, and adaptable

day traders are diligent students of their own performance. Regularly reviewing past trades allows them to identify patterns, strengths, and weaknesses.

# 7 A STRING OF BAD TRADES SHOULDN'T BREAK YOU

The reality of day trading success rests on two steadfast pillars: patience and consistency. In this chapter, we will delve into the profound significance of cultivating patience and maintaining unwavering consistency in your day trading journey. We'll explore how the ebbs and flows of profitability demand a long-term perspective and the unyielding commitment to execute your trading plan with diligence.

### 1. Patience: The Quiet Virtue

In the world of day trading, patience is often the unsung hero. While exhilarating moments may be few and far between, it's the patient trader who knows when to pounce and when to wait. Patience means resisting the urge to chase after every opportunity, allowing trades to develop, and giving the market the time it needs to reveal its intentions. The patient trader understands that success is a marathon, not a sprint.

### 2. Consistency: The Path to Mastery

Consistency is the foundation upon which day trading mastery is built. It's not about hitting the jackpot on a single trade; it's about steadily accumulating wins and minimizing losses over time. Consistency involves adhering to your trading plan with discipline, regardless of market fluctuations or emotional impulses. It's the sum of all your trades that ultimately defines your success, and consistency ensures that each trade contributes positively to your overall performance.

### 3. Weathering the Storms

Not every day in the life of a day trader will be a profitable one. In fact, losses are an inherent part of the game. It's during these challenging moments that patience and consistency shine the brightest. A patient trader doesn't become disheartened by a string of losses but remains focused on the bigger picture. Consistency allows you to ride out the storm, knowing that success is determined by your ability to bounce back and maintain your trading rhythm.

### 4. The Long-Term Perspective

Day trading success is not about quick fixes or overnight riches. It's a journey that requires a long-term perspective. The patient and consistent trader understands that success is measured not by daily gains or losses but by the gradual growth of their trading account over time. By keeping your eyes on the horizon and resisting the allure of instant gratification, you position yourself for sustained success in the dynamic world of day trading.

### 5. Mastering the Art of Self-Discipline

Patience and consistency both draw heavily from the well of self-discipline. This trait allows you to stick to your trading plan even when emotions threaten to sway your decisions. Self-discipline empowers you to remain patient during periods of stagnation and to execute your trades with consistent precision, regardless of market volatility.

# 8 USING TECHNOLOGY TO GET AHEAD

The world of day trading has undergone a remarkable transformation, propelled by the unprecedented capabilities of advanced trading platforms, cutting-edge analytical tools, and real-time data feeds. In this chapter, we embark on a journey to unveil the revolutionary impact of technology on day trading. By delving into real examples, we will explore how embracing these technological advancements empowers day traders to access timely market information, decipher intricate market trends, and execute trades with unparalleled precision. Through this exploration, we aim to demonstrate how technology has become a true game-changer for day traders, offering the potential to turn knowledge into profit.

## The Rise of Advanced Trading Platforms

Gone are the days of bustling trading floors and raucous shouts. Today's day traders wield the power of advanced trading platforms that have ushered in a new era of seamless and efficient trading. These platforms serve as digital battlegrounds where traders access a multitude of tools and features tailored to enhance decision-making. For instance, consider the MetaTrader 4 (MT4) trading platform, which boasts an intuitive user interface and customizable charts. MT4 empowers traders to swiftly navigate market data, identify trends, and pinpoint potential entry and exit points. Moreover, its real-time capabilities provide an invaluable edge, allowing traders to monitor positions, adjust strategies, and execute trades with lightning speed.

## Analytical Tools: Decoding Market Trends

At the heart of successful day trading lies the ability to analyze market trends and patterns.

Advanced analytical tools are the keys to unlocking these insights. Imagine a day trader utilizing Fibonacci retracement levels. This tool, available on platforms like TradingView, helps identify potential price reversal points by analyzing historical price movements. By applying Fibonacci retracement to a recent uptrend, the trader can pinpoint levels at which price corrections may occur, aiding in strategic decision-making.

Furthermore, algorithmic trading systems like MetaTrader 4's Expert Advisors (EAs) automate trading strategies based on predetermined criteria. For instance, a day trader could program an EA to execute trades when specific technical indicators align, such as a moving average crossover. This example showcases how technology-driven analysis can empower day traders to make informed decisions without the constraints of manual execution.

Real-Time Data Feeds: Seizing Opportune Moments

Real-time data feeds are the lifelines that keep day traders ahead of the curve. These feeds provide instantaneous updates on price movements, trading volumes, and breaking news. To illustrate, imagine a day trader closely monitoring a popular stock that is experiencing high volatility due to an earnings report. With a real-time data feed, the trader receives up-to-the-millisecond updates, enabling them to react swiftly to sudden price swings. This real-world example underscores how real-time data feeds are essential for seizing fleeting opportunities and adapting to rapidly evolving market dynamics.

Staying Abreast of Market Information

In the realm of day trading, knowledge translates directly into power. Staying informed about breaking news, economic indicators, and geopolitical events is paramount. Technology empowers day traders to stay updated through various channels. For instance, utilizing news aggregators such as Bloomberg Terminal grants traders access to real-time financial news, earnings reports, and economic data releases. Additionally, social media platforms like Twitter offer curated streams of information from industry experts, providing valuable insights that can influence trading decisions. By utilizing these tools, day traders can remain informed, adapting their strategies to align with the latest market developments.

Embracing Technology: A Catalyst for Success

Embracing technology isn't a mere luxury; it's a strategic imperative that can amplify a day trader's prowess. Integrating advanced tools and real-time data into one's trading routine transforms them into an agile, well-informed, and efficient trader. Consider a day trader utilizing Level II quotes, which display real-time bid and ask prices along with the associated trading volume. This information empowers the trader to gauge market sentiment and make well-informed decisions on order placement. By leveraging technology, the trader optimizes their entry and exit points, capitalizing on market inefficiencies for potential gains.

# 9 THE AGE OF DAY TRADING BOTS

Day trading bots, often referred to as algorithmic trading bots, are software programs that autonomously execute trades in financial markets based on predetermined criteria and strategies. These bots have the capacity to analyze market data, identify patterns, and execute trades at speeds far surpassing human capabilities.

**The Evolution of Automated Trading:** The concept of automated trading dates back decades, but recent technological advancements have made it more accessible and sophisticated than ever before. As computing power increased and real-time data feeds became more prevalent, the development of complex trading algorithms became feasible.

**Types of Day Trading Bots:** Day trading bots can be categorized into several types based on their underlying strategies. These include trend-following bots, mean-reversion bots, arbitrage bots, and sentiment analysis bots. Each type operates on specific principles and utilizes various technical indicators to make trading decisions.

The Mechanics Behind Day Trading Bots

**Algorithmic Strategies and Trading Rules:** Day trading bots operate based on sets of predefined rules and algorithms. These rules encompass technical indicators, price patterns, and other market variables. Traders can design their bots to implement strategies ranging from simple moving average crossovers to intricate machine learning algorithms.

**Real-time Data Integration:** To make informed trading decisions, day trading bots rely on real-time market data. These bots continuously analyze price movements, trading volumes, and other relevant metrics to identify potential opportunities.

**Trade Execution and Management:** Once a trading signal is generated, the bot swiftly executes the trade according to the predetermined parameters. Bots can also manage trades by setting stop-loss and take-profit levels, trailing stops, and adjusting positions based on market conditions.

The Pros of Day Trading Bots

**Speed and Precision:** One of the most significant advantages of day trading bots is their lightning-fast execution. Bots can react to market movements within milliseconds, potentially capitalizing on fleeting opportunities that human traders might miss.

**Elimination of Emotional Bias:** Emotional decision-making can cloud a trader's judgment and lead to impulsive actions. Bots operate based on predefined rules, devoid of emotions, ensuring consistent and disciplined execution of trading strategies.

**Continuous Market Monitoring:** Day trading bots can monitor multiple markets and assets simultaneously, ensuring no potential trade setups are overlooked. This continuous surveillance enables traders to capitalize on a broader range of opportunities.

**Backtesting and Optimization:** Bots allow traders to backtest their strategies using historical data, providing insights into their performance under various market conditions. This feature facilitates strategy refinement and optimization.

Navigating the Challenges

**Over-Reliance on Automation:** While automation can be advantageous, over-reliance on bots without a solid understanding of trading fundamentals can lead to suboptimal outcomes. Traders should view bots as tools that augment their skills rather than replace them.

**Technical Glitches and System Failures:** Bots are not immune to technical glitches or system failures, which can potentially result in erroneous trades or missed opportunities. It's essential to implement safeguards and conduct thorough testing before deploying a bot.

**Market Volatility and Unexpected Events:** Rapid market fluctuations and unexpected events can challenge a bot's ability to adapt. Traders must consider these scenarios and implement risk management measures to mitigate potential losses.

Choosing the Right Bot: Factors to Consider

**Strategy Flexibility:** A well-designed bot should allow traders to implement a wide range of trading strategies and customize parameters to suit their preferences.

**Risk Management Features:** Effective risk management is crucial. Bots should include features such as stop-loss and take-profit orders to protect capital.

**User-Friendly Interface:** An intuitive user interface simplifies bot setup, configuration, and monitoring, making it accessible to traders of all skill levels.

**Backtesting and Performance Analysis:** Bots that offer comprehensive backtesting and performance analysis tools empower traders to assess the viability of their strategies before deploying them in real-time trading.

Day Trading Bots in Action: Real-World Examples

**Fibonacci-based Bots:** These bots utilize the Fibonacci sequence and its ratios to identify potential support and resistance levels, aiding in trade entry and exit decisions.

**Moving Average Crossover Bots:** Based on the crossing of different moving averages, these bots help traders identify trends and potential reversals.

**Arbitrage Bots:** Arbitrage bots exploit price discrepancies between different markets or exchanges, aiming to profit from the price differentials.

**Sentiment Analysis Bots:** Leveraging natural language processing and sentiment analysis, these bots analyze news and social media sentiment to gauge market sentiment and trends.

Regulatory and Ethical Considerations

**Regulatory Landscape:** The use of day trading bots is subject to regulatory oversight in various jurisdictions. Traders should ensure compliance with relevant laws and regulations.

**Fair Competition and Market Integrity:** The proliferation of bots raises questions about market fairness and manipulation. Regulatory bodies and exchanges aim to maintain a level playing field and prevent unfair advantages.

The Future of Day Trading: Human vs. Machine

**Coexistence of Traders and Bots:** The future likely holds a landscape where human traders and bots coexist, each contributing unique strengths to the trading process.

**Impact on Trading Psychology and Skill Development:** While bots can eliminate emotional biases, they also challenge traders to evolve their skill sets, focusing on strategy development and risk management.

**Evolution of Bot Capabilities:** As technology advances, day trading bots will likely become more sophisticated, incorporating advanced machine learning and artificial intelligence techniques.

# 10 THE 1% ELITE DAY TRADERS HAVE INTUITION

Intuition, often described as a gut feeling or a sixth sense, is an innate and immediate understanding that transcends conscious reasoning. In the context of day trading, it's the instinctive hunch or insight that arises beyond the realm of numerical analysis. It's not a mystical force but rather a result of the brain's ability to process vast amounts of information at a subconscious level, honed through experience and knowledge.

The Role of Intuition in Decision-Making

In the realm of day trading, where every decision can have significant financial implications, the role of intuition is both subtle and profound.

Cultivating Intuition in Day Traders

Nurturing intuition is a process that evolves over time and requires conscious effort.

Intuition vs. Emotion: Drawing the Line

While intuition is a valuable asset, it's crucial to differentiate it from emotional decision-making.

When Intuition Guided Successful Trades

Intuition as a Tool, Not a Replacement

Navigating Uncertainty with Intuition

# KEEPING A JOURNAL

If you want to survive the long run as a day trader and make enough and much more than your job than you need to maintain a journal and write down all the trades you are taking and the reasoning behind that.

You need this so you can make a habit of perfecting your craft and continuously taking better decisions and this is the process that will put you in the top 1% of traders and probably in the top 0.1% traders if you keep on learning everyday, if you keep on perfecting your craft, focus on eliminating mistakes and bad decisions.

# JOIN US AND GET AHEAD

If you would like to be part of an exclusive group who are reaching new heights through collaborative force and synergy then email me at **jain440540@gmail.com** and get started right away.

You will be part of an exclusive group where you will keep receiving up to date information, tips and trades that we are taking, you can share your story, get one on one help and get to speed fast.

Also currently I am taking several one on ones and setting new traders for a fee of 1000$ and we are day trading on ByBit.com and TickMill.com You can also join us and get 30% off on my one on one day trading courses by simply giving a nice review and sharing the screenshot at the above email. If you really want maximum progress connect with me and I will put you on the most profitable path and help you quit the 9-5 forever. Me and my students are taking high probability trades which have a success rate of over 65% and an edge that beats the trading fees and manages a nice return on the money. I can guarantee that you will make at least 2% of your capital easily, if you have 10,000$ by investing just 2 hours daily you will be able to earn 200$ easily from the markets and in a month that is 6000$ and if you have more capital then you will make huge, you don't need to trust anyone with the money I will give you the keys so that you will be able to put in the orders with peace of mind and realize immense profits. Email me today at jain440540@gmail.com to get started! I will give you personal phone number where you can WhatsApp and get up to speed. +91-9172440540 I may not be able to respond to all emails but my WhatsApp remains active. Positive reviews are important to me so please do write a positive review first and then message me with the screenshot and I will help you.

Thank You!

Vaibhav Jain